50 Rice Dishes from Around the World Recipes

By: Kelly Johnson

Table of Contents

- Spanish Paella
- Indian Biryani
- Chinese Fried Rice
- Japanese Sushi Rice
- Italian Risotto
- Persian Polo
- Mexican Arroz con Pollo
- Thai Pineapple Fried Rice
- Caribbean Jollof Rice
- Egyptian Koshari
- Indonesian Nasi Goreng
- Sri Lankan Coconut Rice
- Malaysian Nasi Lemak
- Greek Pilaf
- Korean Bibimbap
- Middle Eastern Pilaf with Lamb
- Lebanese Mujadara
- Cajun Jambalaya
- Vietnamese Com tam (Broken Rice)
- Turkish Pilav with Chickpeas
- Portuguese Arroz de Marisco
- Brazilian Baked Rice
- French Riz de Veau (Veal with Rice)
- Burmese Shan Rice
- Ethiopian Berbere Rice
- Afghan Sheer Kebab Rice
- Moroccan Vegetable Couscous
- Caribbean Rice and Beans
- Filipino Sinangag (Garlic Fried Rice)
- South African Biryani
- Afghan Pilaf with Dried Fruits
- Jamaican Rice and Peas
- Palestinian Maqluba
- Pakistani Pulao
- Tanzanian Coconut Rice

- Italian Arancini (Rice Balls)
- Algerian Mechoui Rice
- Thai Sticky Rice with Mango
- Egyptian Mahshi (Stuffed Rice)
- Cambodian Fried Rice
- Iranian Tahchin
- Dominican Mangu with Rice
- Senegalese Thiéboudienne
- Indian Lemon Rice
- Guatemalan Arroz con Pollo
- Turkish Rice with Spices
- Chinese Sticky Rice Dumplings
- Malaysian Sambal Rice
- Syrian Rice Pilaf
- Ukrainian Rice with Mushrooms

Spanish Paella

Ingredients:

- 2 tbsp olive oil
- 1 onion, chopped
- 1 bell pepper, chopped
- 2 garlic cloves, minced
- 1 ½ cups short-grain rice (such as Arborio)
- 3 cups chicken or vegetable broth
- 1 tsp smoked paprika
- ½ tsp saffron threads (optional)
- 1 cup diced tomatoes
- 1 ½ cups peas (frozen or fresh)
- 1 lb mixed seafood (shrimp, mussels, clams)
- 1 cup cooked chicken, shredded (optional)
- Lemon wedges for serving

Instructions:

1. Heat olive oil in a large skillet or paella pan over medium heat. Add onion, bell pepper, and garlic. Sauté until soft, about 5 minutes.
2. Stir in rice, paprika, and saffron (if using), then add diced tomatoes and broth. Bring to a simmer.
3. Cover and cook for 15-20 minutes, adding peas and stirring occasionally.
4. Once the rice is nearly cooked, arrange the seafood (and chicken if using) on top. Cover and cook for an additional 5-7 minutes, or until the seafood is cooked through.
5. Serve with lemon wedges.

Indian Biryani

Ingredients:

- 2 cups basmati rice, soaked for 30 minutes
- 1 lb chicken, beef, or lamb (cubed)
- 2 tbsp vegetable oil
- 1 onion, thinly sliced
- 2 garlic cloves, minced
- 1-inch piece of ginger, grated
- 2 tbsp biryani masala
- ½ tsp turmeric
- 1 tsp garam masala
- 1 tsp cumin
- 1 tsp coriander
- 2 cups yogurt
- 1 cup fried onions
- Fresh cilantro and mint leaves
- 3 cups water

Instructions:

1. Heat oil in a large pot. Sauté onion, garlic, and ginger until fragrant.
2. Add the meat and cook until browned. Stir in the spices and cook for 2 minutes.
3. Add yogurt and fried onions, then mix well. Let it simmer for 10 minutes.
4. In another pot, bring water to a boil and add the soaked rice. Cook until the rice is 70% done, then drain.
5. Layer the cooked rice on top of the meat mixture. Cover and cook on low heat for 20 minutes to allow the flavors to meld.
6. Garnish with fresh cilantro and mint before serving.

Chinese Fried Rice

Ingredients:

- 3 cups cooked rice (preferably day-old)
- 2 tbsp vegetable oil
- 2 eggs, lightly beaten
- 1 onion, chopped
- 2 garlic cloves, minced
- 1 cup mixed vegetables (peas, carrots, corn)
- 2 tbsp soy sauce
- 1 tsp sesame oil
- Green onions, chopped for garnish

Instructions:

1. Heat vegetable oil in a large pan or wok over medium heat. Scramble the eggs in the pan until cooked, then remove and set aside.
2. Add onions and garlic to the same pan, cooking until soft. Stir in the mixed vegetables and cook for another 2 minutes.
3. Add rice, soy sauce, and sesame oil, stirring to combine.
4. Return the cooked eggs to the pan and toss everything together.
5. Garnish with green onions and serve.

Japanese Sushi Rice

Ingredients:

- 2 cups short-grain sushi rice
- 2 cups water
- ¼ cup rice vinegar
- 2 tbsp sugar
- 1 tsp salt

Instructions:

1. Rinse sushi rice under cold water until the water runs clear.
2. In a pot, bring rice and water to a boil, then reduce to a simmer. Cover and cook for 20 minutes.
3. In a small bowl, mix rice vinegar, sugar, and salt until dissolved.
4. Once rice is cooked, transfer it to a flat pan and drizzle with vinegar mixture. Gently fold the rice to mix, then allow it to cool to room temperature.

Italian Risotto

Ingredients:

- 1 ½ cups Arborio rice
- 4 cups chicken or vegetable broth, warmed
- 2 tbsp olive oil
- 1 onion, chopped
- 2 garlic cloves, minced
- ½ cup dry white wine
- ½ cup Parmesan cheese, grated
- Fresh parsley, chopped for garnish

Instructions:

1. Heat olive oil in a large pan over medium heat. Add onion and garlic and cook until softened.
2. Stir in the rice and cook for 1-2 minutes.
3. Add wine and let it absorb into the rice.
4. Gradually add broth, one ladle at a time, stirring frequently. Let each addition absorb before adding more. Continue until the rice is tender and creamy, about 18-20 minutes.
5. Stir in Parmesan cheese and garnish with parsley.

Persian Polo

Ingredients:

- 2 cups basmati rice
- 1 lb lamb, chicken, or beef (cubed)
- 2 tbsp vegetable oil
- 1 onion, chopped
- 2 garlic cloves, minced
- 1 tsp turmeric
- 1 tsp cinnamon
- 1 cup yogurt
- ½ cup raisins
- ¼ cup slivered almonds

Instructions:

1. Heat oil in a pot. Sauté onion and garlic until golden.
2. Add the meat and brown on all sides. Stir in turmeric and cinnamon.
3. Add yogurt, raisins, and almonds, mixing well.
4. In another pot, cook rice according to package instructions.
5. Layer the cooked rice over the meat mixture, cover, and cook on low for 20 minutes.
6. Serve with a sprinkle of additional raisins and almonds.

Mexican Arroz con Pollo

Ingredients:

- 1 lb chicken, cut into pieces
- 1 cup long-grain rice
- 2 tbsp olive oil
- 1 onion, chopped
- 2 garlic cloves, minced
- 1 can diced tomatoes (14 oz)
- 2 cups chicken broth
- 1 tsp cumin
- 1 tsp chili powder
- 1 cup peas and carrots (frozen or fresh)

Instructions:

1. Heat oil in a large pan. Brown the chicken on all sides, then remove and set aside.
2. In the same pan, sauté onion and garlic until softened. Stir in rice, tomatoes, chicken broth, cumin, and chili powder.
3. Return the chicken to the pan and bring to a boil. Cover and reduce to a simmer for 20 minutes.
4. Stir in peas and carrots and cook for an additional 5 minutes.
5. Serve the chicken over the rice.

Thai Pineapple Fried Rice

Ingredients:

- 3 cups cooked jasmine rice
- 1 tbsp vegetable oil
- 1 onion, chopped
- 1 cup diced pineapple
- 2 garlic cloves, minced
- 1 red bell pepper, chopped
- 1 tsp curry powder
- 2 tbsp soy sauce
- 1 tsp fish sauce
- 1 egg, scrambled
- Green onions and cilantro for garnish

Instructions:

1. Heat oil in a wok. Add onion, garlic, and bell pepper. Stir-fry for 2-3 minutes.
2. Add pineapple and cook for another 2 minutes.
3. Stir in the rice, curry powder, soy sauce, and fish sauce.
4. Push the rice to one side of the pan and scramble the egg on the other side. Combine everything together.
5. Garnish with green onions and cilantro before serving.

Caribbean Jollof Rice

Ingredients:

- 2 cups long-grain parboiled rice
- 3 tbsp vegetable oil
- 1 onion, chopped
- 2 garlic cloves, minced
- 1 can diced tomatoes (14 oz)
- 1 tsp thyme
- 1 tsp paprika
- 1 tsp curry powder
- 2 cups chicken broth
- 1 cup mixed vegetables (peas, carrots, corn)

Instructions:

1. Heat oil in a large pot. Add onion and garlic and sauté until softened.
2. Stir in diced tomatoes, thyme, paprika, and curry powder. Cook for 5 minutes.
3. Add rice, chicken broth, and mixed vegetables. Bring to a boil, then reduce heat to low and cover.
4. Cook for 20-25 minutes, or until the rice is tender and the liquid has been absorbed.
5. Serve with your choice of protein.

Egyptian Koshari

Ingredients:

- 1 cup rice
- 1 cup lentils (green or brown)
- 1 cup macaroni pasta (small)
- 2 onions, thinly sliced
- 2 tbsp vegetable oil
- 2 garlic cloves, minced
- 1 can (14 oz) crushed tomatoes
- 1 tsp ground cumin
- 1 tsp ground coriander
- Salt and pepper to taste
- Vinegar, to taste

Instructions:

1. Cook the rice and lentils separately according to package instructions. Cook the macaroni and set aside.
2. In a large pan, heat oil and fry the sliced onions until crispy. Remove half of the onions and set aside for garnish.
3. In the same pan, sauté garlic and spices, then add the crushed tomatoes and simmer for 10 minutes.
4. Mix the rice, lentils, and macaroni together in a large serving bowl. Pour the tomato sauce over and toss to combine.
5. Garnish with crispy onions and drizzle with vinegar before serving.

Indonesian Nasi Goreng

Ingredients:

- 3 cups cooked jasmine rice (preferably day-old)
- 2 tbsp vegetable oil
- 2 garlic cloves, minced
- 1 shallot, finely chopped
- 2 eggs, beaten
- 1 cup cooked chicken or shrimp (optional)
- 2 tbsp soy sauce
- 1 tbsp sweet soy sauce (kecap manis)
- 1 tsp chili paste (optional)
- 1 cup mixed vegetables (carrots, peas, corn)
- Green onions, chopped for garnish

Instructions:

1. Heat oil in a wok. Add garlic and shallots and sauté until fragrant.
2. Add the eggs and scramble them in the wok.
3. Stir in the chicken or shrimp, soy sauce, sweet soy sauce, and chili paste.
4. Add the mixed vegetables and cook for 2 minutes.
5. Add the cooked rice, breaking up any clumps. Stir-fry for 5-7 minutes, allowing the flavors to combine.
6. Garnish with chopped green onions before serving.

Sri Lankan Coconut Rice

Ingredients:

- 2 cups basmati rice
- 2 cups coconut milk
- 1 cup water
- 1 cinnamon stick
- 2 cloves
- 1 cardamom pod
- 1 tbsp mustard seeds
- 2 tbsp vegetable oil
- 2 curry leaves (optional)
- Salt to taste

Instructions:

1. Rinse the rice and drain.
2. In a large saucepan, heat oil and add mustard seeds, cinnamon stick, cloves, cardamom, and curry leaves. Fry until fragrant.
3. Add the rice and cook for 2 minutes in the spices.
4. Pour in coconut milk, water, and salt, then bring to a boil.
5. Lower the heat, cover, and simmer for 15-20 minutes or until rice is cooked and the liquid is absorbed.

Malaysian Nasi Lemak

Ingredients:

- 2 cups jasmine rice
- 1 cup coconut milk
- 2 cups water
- 1 pandan leaf (optional)
- 2 tbsp vegetable oil
- 2 boiled eggs, halved
- ½ cup roasted peanuts
- ½ cup sambal (chili paste)
- 1 cucumber, sliced

Instructions:

1. Rinse the rice, then cook with coconut milk, water, and pandan leaf if available, in a rice cooker or saucepan.
2. While the rice cooks, fry the peanuts in oil until crispy.
3. Once the rice is done, fluff it and serve with sambal, boiled eggs, peanuts, and cucumber slices.
4. Garnish with fresh herbs if desired.

Greek Pilaf

Ingredients:

- 1 ½ cups long-grain rice
- 2 tbsp olive oil
- 1 onion, chopped
- 2 garlic cloves, minced
- 2 cups chicken broth
- 1 bay leaf
- 1 tsp dried oregano
- Salt and pepper to taste
- Fresh parsley, chopped for garnish

Instructions:

1. Heat olive oil in a large pan. Add onion and garlic, sautéing until softened.
2. Stir in the rice and cook for 1-2

minutes, allowing the rice to lightly toast.
3. Add the chicken broth, bay leaf, oregano, salt, and pepper. Bring to a boil, then reduce heat and cover.
4. Simmer for about 15-20 minutes until the rice is tender and the liquid is absorbed.
5. Garnish with fresh parsley before serving.

Korean Bibimbap

Ingredients:

- 2 cups cooked rice (preferably short-grain)
- 1 carrot, julienned
- 1 zucchini, julienned
- 1 cup spinach, blanched
- 4-5 shiitake mushrooms, sliced
- 1 egg (fried sunny side up)
- 2 tbsp gochujang (Korean chili paste)
- 1 tbsp sesame oil
- 1 tbsp sesame seeds
- Soy sauce to taste
- Garlic, minced

Instructions:

1. Sauté the vegetables separately in sesame oil, seasoning with a pinch of salt and soy sauce.
2. Fry the egg sunny side up.
3. To assemble, place rice in a bowl and top with the sautéed vegetables and fried egg.
4. Drizzle with gochujang, sesame oil, and a sprinkle of sesame seeds.
5. Mix everything together before eating.

Middle Eastern Pilaf with Lamb

Ingredients:

- 2 cups basmati rice
- 1 lb lamb, cubed
- 1 onion, chopped
- 3 garlic cloves, minced
- 1 tbsp ground cumin
- 1 tsp cinnamon
- 2 cups chicken broth
- 1 tbsp olive oil
- 1 cup dried apricots, chopped
- Salt and pepper to taste
- Fresh cilantro for garnish

Instructions:

1. In a large pot, heat olive oil and brown the lamb cubes. Remove and set aside.
2. In the same pot, sauté the onion and garlic until soft.
3. Stir in cumin and cinnamon, then return the lamb to the pot.
4. Add the rice, apricots, and chicken broth. Bring to a boil, then cover and simmer for 20-25 minutes until the rice is tender.
5. Garnish with fresh cilantro and serve.

Lebanese Mujadara

Ingredients:

- 1 cup lentils
- 1 cup rice
- 2 onions, sliced
- 2 tbsp olive oil
- 1 tsp ground cumin
- 1 tsp ground coriander
- Salt and pepper to taste
- Fresh parsley for garnish

Instructions:

1. Cook the lentils in water until tender (about 20-25 minutes). Drain and set aside.
2. Cook the rice according to package instructions.
3. In a pan, heat olive oil and fry the onions until caramelized.
4. Combine the rice, lentils, and spices in a large bowl, then top with the caramelized onions.
5. Garnish with fresh parsley before serving.

Cajun Jambalaya

Ingredients:

- 2 cups rice
- 1 lb chicken breast, diced
- 1 lb shrimp, peeled and deveined
- 1 onion, chopped
- 1 bell pepper, chopped
- 2 celery stalks, chopped
- 2 garlic cloves, minced
- 1 can (14 oz) diced tomatoes
- 1 tsp paprika
- 1 tsp thyme
- 1 tsp cayenne pepper
- 4 cups chicken broth
- Salt and pepper to taste
- Green onions for garnish

Instructions:

1. In a large pot, sauté onion, bell pepper, celery, and garlic until softened.
2. Add the chicken and cook until browned.
3. Stir in tomatoes, spices, and chicken broth. Bring to a boil, then reduce heat to simmer.
4. Add rice and cook for 20-25 minutes until the rice is tender.
5. Add shrimp and cook until pink and cooked through.
6. Garnish with green onions before serving.

Vietnamese Com tam (Broken Rice)

Ingredients:

- 2 cups broken rice
- 1 pork chop, marinated and grilled
- 1 fried egg
- Pickled vegetables (carrot and daikon)
- Cucumber slices
- Fresh cilantro

Instructions:

1. Cook the broken rice according to package instructions.
2. Grill or pan-fry the marinated pork chop until cooked through.
3. Fry an egg sunny side up.
4. Serve the rice with the pork chop, egg, pickled vegetables, cucumber slices, and a sprinkle of cilantro.
5. Enjoy with a drizzle of soy sauce or fish sauce.

Turkish Pilav with Chickpeas

Ingredients:

- 2 cups long-grain rice
- 1 cup cooked chickpeas (or canned)
- 1 onion, chopped
- 2 tbsp olive oil
- 1 cinnamon stick
- 2 cloves
- 2 cups chicken or vegetable broth
- Salt and pepper to taste
- Fresh parsley for garnish

Instructions:

1. Rinse the rice and set it aside.
2. In a large pot, heat olive oil and sauté the onion until soft.
3. Add the cinnamon stick, cloves, and rice, stirring to coat the rice with oil.
4. Pour in the broth and bring it to a boil. Reduce the heat, cover, and simmer for 15-20 minutes, until the rice is tender.
5. Stir in the chickpeas and cook for another 5 minutes.
6. Garnish with fresh parsley and serve.

Portuguese Arroz de Marisco

Ingredients:

- 2 cups short-grain rice
- 1 lb mixed seafood (shrimp, clams, mussels, squid)
- 1 onion, chopped
- 2 garlic cloves, minced
- 1 bell pepper, chopped
- 2 tomatoes, chopped
- 1 cup white wine
- 4 cups seafood broth
- 1 tsp paprika
- 1 tsp saffron (optional)
- 2 tbsp olive oil
- Fresh cilantro for garnish

Instructions:

1. Heat olive oil in a large pot and sauté onion, garlic, and bell pepper until soft.
2. Add chopped tomatoes, paprika, and saffron, then cook for another 5 minutes.
3. Stir in the rice, ensuring it's coated with the sauce.
4. Pour in the white wine and seafood broth, bring to a boil, and reduce to a simmer.
5. Add the seafood and cook until the rice is tender and the seafood is cooked through (about 10 minutes).
6. Garnish with fresh cilantro and serve.

Brazilian Baked Rice

Ingredients:

- 2 cups long-grain rice
- 4 cups chicken broth
- 1 onion, chopped
- 2 garlic cloves, minced
- 2 tbsp olive oil
- 1 cup diced tomatoes
- 1 cup grated Parmesan cheese
- Salt and pepper to taste

Instructions:

1. Preheat the oven to 350°F (175°C).
2. In a large pan, heat olive oil and sauté onion and garlic until soft.
3. Stir in the tomatoes and cook for 5 minutes.
4. Add the rice and chicken broth, season with salt and pepper, and bring to a boil.
5. Transfer the mixture to a baking dish, cover, and bake for 25 minutes.
6. Remove from the oven, sprinkle with Parmesan cheese, and bake uncovered for an additional 10 minutes.
7. Serve hot and enjoy!

French Riz de Veau (Veal with Rice)

Ingredients:

- 1 lb veal stew meat, cubed
- 1 cup long-grain rice
- 2 tbsp butter
- 1 onion, chopped
- 1 carrot, diced
- 2 garlic cloves, minced
- 2 cups beef or veal stock
- 1 bay leaf
- Fresh thyme
- Salt and pepper to taste

Instructions:

1. Heat butter in a large pot and brown the veal cubes on all sides.
2. Remove the veal and set it aside. In the same pot, sauté onion, carrot, and garlic until softened.
3. Add the rice and stir to coat it with the butter.
4. Pour in the stock, bay leaf, and thyme, and bring it to a boil.
5. Add the veal back into the pot, cover, and simmer for 20-25 minutes until the rice and veal are tender.
6. Season with salt and pepper and serve.

Burmese Shan Rice

Ingredients:

- 2 cups jasmine rice
- 1 lb chicken thighs, boneless and skinless
- 2 tbsp vegetable oil
- 1 onion, chopped
- 2 garlic cloves, minced
- 1 tbsp ginger, grated
- 1 tbsp turmeric powder
- 1 tsp ground cumin
- 2 cups chicken broth
- 1 cup coconut milk
- 1 tbsp fish sauce
- Salt and pepper to taste
- Fresh cilantro for garnish

Instructions:

1. Heat vegetable oil in a large pan and sauté onion, garlic, and ginger until fragrant.
2. Add the chicken thighs and brown on both sides.
3. Stir in turmeric, cumin, and rice, cooking for 2 minutes.
4. Add the chicken broth, coconut milk, fish sauce, salt, and pepper, and bring to a boil.
5. Cover and simmer for 20 minutes, until the rice and chicken are fully cooked.
6. Garnish with fresh cilantro and serve.

Ethiopian Berbere Rice

Ingredients:

- 2 cups basmati rice
- 1 tbsp berbere spice mix (or more to taste)
- 2 tbsp olive oil
- 1 onion, chopped
- 2 garlic cloves, minced
- 2 cups vegetable broth
- 1 can (14 oz) diced tomatoes
- Salt to taste
- Fresh cilantro for garnish

Instructions:

1. Rinse the rice and set it aside.
2. In a large pot, heat olive oil and sauté onion and garlic until softened.
3. Stir in the berbere spice mix and cook for 1-2 minutes.
4. Add the diced tomatoes, vegetable broth, and rice, bringing it to a boil.
5. Lower the heat, cover, and simmer for 20 minutes until the rice is cooked.
6. Garnish with fresh cilantro and serve.

Afghan Sheer Kebab Rice

Ingredients:

- 2 cups basmati rice
- 1 lb ground lamb or beef
- 1 onion, finely chopped
- 2 garlic cloves, minced
- 1 tsp ground coriander
- 1 tsp ground cumin
- 1 tsp turmeric
- 1 tsp cinnamon
- 1 tbsp vegetable oil
- 2 cups beef broth
- Salt and pepper to taste
- Fresh mint for garnish

Instructions:

1. Cook the rice according to package instructions and set aside.
2. In a pan, heat oil and sauté onion and garlic until softened.
3. Add the ground lamb or beef, spices, salt, and pepper, and cook until browned.
4. Stir in the beef broth and simmer for 10-15 minutes.
5. Serve the meat mixture over the rice, garnished with fresh mint.

Moroccan Vegetable Couscous

Ingredients:

- 2 cups couscous
- 1 zucchini, diced
- 1 carrot, diced
- 1 onion, chopped
- 1 bell pepper, chopped
- 1 can (14 oz) chickpeas, drained and rinsed
- 2 tbsp olive oil
- 1 tsp ground cumin
- 1 tsp paprika
- 1 tsp ground cinnamon
- 2 cups vegetable broth
- Salt and pepper to taste
- Fresh parsley for garnish

Instructions:

1. Heat olive oil in a large pot and sauté the onion, bell pepper, zucchini, and carrot until softened.
2. Stir in the cumin, paprika, and cinnamon, and cook for 2 minutes.
3. Add the chickpeas and vegetable broth, bringing to a boil.
4. Stir in the couscous, cover, and let it steam for 5-10 minutes.
5. Fluff the couscous and serve, garnished with fresh parsley.

Caribbean Rice and Beans

Ingredients:

- 2 cups long-grain rice
- 1 can (15 oz) red kidney beans, drained and rinsed
- 1 onion, chopped
- 2 garlic cloves, minced
- 1 bell pepper, chopped
- 1 tsp thyme
- 1 tsp allspice
- 1 can (14 oz) coconut milk
- 2 cups water
- Salt and pepper to taste
- Fresh cilantro for garnish

Instructions:

1. In a large pot, sauté onion, garlic, and bell pepper until soft.
2. Add the thyme, allspice, rice, beans, coconut milk, and water. Bring to a boil.
3. Reduce heat, cover, and simmer for 20-25 minutes until the rice is cooked and the liquid is absorbed.
4. Garnish with fresh cilantro before serving.

Filipino Sinangag (Garlic Fried Rice)

Ingredients:

- 4 cups cooked white rice (preferably day-old)
- 4 garlic cloves, minced
- 2 tbsp vegetable oil
- 2 eggs (optional)
- 2 green onions, chopped
- Salt and pepper to taste

Instructions:

1. Heat vegetable oil in a large skillet or wok.
2. Add the garlic and sauté until fragrant, about 2 minutes.
3. Add the cooked rice, breaking up any clumps, and stir to coat the rice with garlic.
4. Stir-fry for 5-7 minutes until the rice is lightly browned and heated through.
5. If desired, scramble eggs in a separate pan and mix them into the rice.
6. Season with salt and pepper, and garnish with green onions before serving.

South African Biryani

Ingredients:

- 2 cups basmati rice
- 1 lb chicken thighs, boneless and skinless, cut into pieces
- 2 onions, thinly sliced
- 4 garlic cloves, minced
- 1 tbsp ginger, minced
- 2 tomatoes, chopped
- 2 tbsp curry powder
- 1 tsp cumin
- 1 tsp coriander
- 2 cups chicken broth
- 1 cup plain yogurt
- 1 tbsp garam masala
- 2 tbsp vegetable oil
- Salt to taste
- Fresh cilantro for garnish

Instructions:

1. Heat oil in a large pot and sauté onions, garlic, and ginger until soft and golden.
2. Add the chicken pieces and cook until browned on all sides.
3. Stir in curry powder, cumin, coriander, and tomatoes, cooking for 2-3 minutes.
4. Add the rice, chicken broth, yogurt, and garam masala, and bring to a boil.
5. Lower the heat, cover, and simmer for 20-25 minutes, until the rice is cooked and the chicken is tender.
6. Garnish with fresh cilantro and serve.

Afghan Pilaf with Dried Fruits

Ingredients:

- 2 cups basmati rice
- 1 lb lamb or chicken, cut into cubes
- 1 onion, chopped
- 1 tsp ground cumin
- 1 tsp ground cinnamon
- 1/2 tsp ground cardamom
- 1 cup mixed dried fruits (apricots, raisins, and prunes)
- 2 cups chicken or vegetable broth
- 2 tbsp vegetable oil
- Salt and pepper to taste
- Fresh parsley for garnish

Instructions:

1. Heat oil in a large pot and sauté onion until soft.
2. Add the lamb or chicken and brown on all sides.
3. Stir in the cumin, cinnamon, cardamom, salt, and pepper, then cook for 1-2 minutes.
4. Add the rice, dried fruits, and broth, and bring to a boil.
5. Cover, reduce heat, and simmer for 20 minutes until the rice is cooked.
6. Garnish with fresh parsley and serve.

Jamaican Rice and Peas

Ingredients:

- 2 cups long-grain rice
- 1 can (15 oz) red kidney beans, drained and rinsed
- 1 cup coconut milk
- 2 cups water
- 1 onion, chopped
- 2 garlic cloves, minced
- 1 tsp thyme
- 1 tsp allspice
- 1 Scotch bonnet pepper (optional, for heat)
- Salt to taste

Instructions:

1. In a large pot, sauté onion and garlic until soft.
2. Add the kidney beans, thyme, allspice, and Scotch bonnet pepper (if using).
3. Pour in the coconut milk, water, and rice. Bring to a boil.
4. Reduce the heat, cover, and simmer for 20-25 minutes until the rice is cooked and the liquid is absorbed.
5. Fluff the rice and serve.

Palestinian Maqluba

Ingredients:

- 2 cups basmati rice
- 1 lb chicken, cut into pieces
- 2 eggplants, sliced
- 2 tomatoes, chopped
- 1 onion, chopped
- 2 garlic cloves, minced
- 1 tsp ground cumin
- 1 tsp ground coriander
- 1 tsp ground cinnamon
- 1/2 tsp turmeric
- 3 cups chicken broth
- 2 tbsp vegetable oil
- Salt and pepper to taste
- Fresh parsley for garnish

Instructions:

1. In a large pot, heat oil and sauté onions and garlic until softened.
2. Add the chicken pieces and cook until browned.
3. Stir in cumin, coriander, cinnamon, turmeric, salt, and pepper.
4. Add the tomatoes and cook for 5 minutes, then pour in the chicken broth.
5. Layer the eggplant slices over the chicken mixture, followed by the rice.
6. Cover and simmer for 30 minutes, then carefully invert the pot onto a serving platter to serve.

Pakistani Pulao

Ingredients:

- 2 cups basmati rice
- 1 lb chicken, cut into pieces
- 2 onions, thinly sliced
- 2 tomatoes, chopped
- 4 garlic cloves, minced
- 1 tbsp ginger, minced
- 1 tbsp ground cumin
- 1 tsp ground coriander
- 1/2 tsp ground turmeric
- 2 cups chicken broth
- 1 tbsp ghee or vegetable oil
- Fresh cilantro for garnish

Instructions:

1. Heat ghee or oil in a large pot and sauté onions until golden brown.
2. Add garlic, ginger, and chicken, cooking until browned.
3. Stir in cumin, coriander, turmeric, and tomatoes, and cook for 5 minutes.
4. Add the rice and chicken broth, bring to a boil, then lower the heat, cover, and simmer for 20-25 minutes.
5. Garnish with fresh cilantro and serve.

Tanzanian Coconut Rice

Ingredients:

- 2 cups basmati rice
- 1 cup coconut milk
- 2 cups water
- 1 onion, chopped
- 1 tsp ginger, grated
- 1 tsp ground cumin
- 1/2 tsp ground cardamom
- Salt to taste
- Fresh cilantro for garnish

Instructions:

1. Heat a pot over medium heat and sauté onion and ginger until softened.
2. Stir in the cumin and cardamom, cooking for 1 minute.
3. Add the rice, coconut milk, water, and salt, bringing it to a boil.
4. Cover, reduce heat, and simmer for 20-25 minutes until the rice is cooked.
5. Garnish with fresh cilantro and serve.

Italian Arancini (Rice Balls)

Ingredients:

- 2 cups cooked risotto rice (preferably day-old)
- 1/2 cup grated Parmesan cheese
- 1/2 cup mozzarella cheese, cubed
- 1 egg
- 1/2 cup breadcrumbs
- 1/2 cup all-purpose flour
- Vegetable oil for frying
- Salt and pepper to taste

Instructions:

1. Mix the cooked rice with Parmesan cheese, egg, and a pinch of salt and pepper.
2. Form the rice mixture into small balls and stuff each with a cube of mozzarella.
3. Roll the rice balls in flour, then dip in beaten egg, and coat with breadcrumbs.
4. Heat oil in a deep fryer or large pot and fry the rice balls until golden brown.
5. Drain on paper towels and serve hot.

Algerian Mechoui Rice

Ingredients:

- 2 cups long-grain rice
- 1 lb lamb, cut into cubes
- 1 onion, chopped
- 2 garlic cloves, minced
- 1 tsp ground cumin
- 1 tsp ground coriander
- 1 tsp paprika
- 2 cups vegetable broth
- 1/2 cup almonds, toasted
- Salt and pepper to taste
- Fresh cilantro for garnish

Instructions:

1. In a large pot, sauté onion and garlic in oil until softened.
2. Add the lamb and brown on all sides.
3. Stir in cumin, coriander, paprika, salt, and pepper, and cook for 1-2 minutes.
4. Add the rice and vegetable broth, bring to a boil.
5. Cover, reduce heat, and simmer for 20-25 minutes.
6. Garnish with toasted almonds and fresh cilantro before serving.

Thai Sticky Rice with Mango

Ingredients:

- 2 cups sticky rice (also called glutinous or sweet rice)
- 1 1/2 cups coconut milk
- 1/2 cup sugar
- 1/4 tsp salt
- 2 ripe mangoes, peeled and sliced

Instructions:

1. Rinse the sticky rice until the water runs clear, then soak it in water for about 1-2 hours.
2. Steam the soaked rice for 30-40 minutes until tender and fully cooked.
3. In a saucepan, heat the coconut milk, sugar, and salt over medium heat, stirring until the sugar dissolves.
4. Pour the coconut mixture over the steamed rice and gently mix to combine. Let it sit for 10-15 minutes.
5. Serve the sticky rice with fresh mango slices on the side or on top.

Egyptian Mahshi (Stuffed Rice)

Ingredients:

- 2 cups short-grain rice, soaked for 30 minutes
- 1 lb ground lamb or beef
- 1 onion, finely chopped
- 1/2 cup fresh parsley, chopped
- 2 tbsp tomato paste
- 1 tsp cinnamon
- 1/2 tsp allspice
- 2 tbsp pine nuts, toasted
- 2 zucchinis or grape leaves for stuffing
- 1 cup tomato sauce
- Salt and pepper to taste

Instructions:

1. Cook the rice until half done. Drain and set aside.
2. In a skillet, sauté onions until soft, then add the ground meat and cook until browned.
3. Stir in parsley, tomato paste, cinnamon, allspice, salt, and pepper. Mix in the cooked rice and pine nuts.
4. Stuff the zucchinis or grape leaves with the rice mixture.
5. Arrange the stuffed vegetables in a pot, cover with tomato sauce, and add enough water to just cover the vegetables.
6. Cover and simmer for 45-60 minutes until fully cooked and tender.

Cambodian Fried Rice

Ingredients:

- 2 cups cooked jasmine rice (preferably day-old rice)
- 1/2 lb chicken, shrimp, or tofu, diced
- 1 onion, finely chopped
- 2 garlic cloves, minced
- 1 egg, lightly beaten
- 1/2 cup peas and carrots, frozen or fresh
- 2 tbsp soy sauce
- 1 tbsp oyster sauce
- 1 tsp sugar
- 1 tbsp vegetable oil
- Fresh cilantro, chopped, for garnish

Instructions:

1. Heat oil in a wok or large skillet over medium-high heat.
2. Add the chicken, shrimp, or tofu and cook until browned.
3. Add the onion and garlic and cook for another 2-3 minutes until fragrant.
4. Push the ingredients to one side and scramble the egg on the other side.
5. Add the rice, peas, and carrots, and stir well.
6. Stir in the soy sauce, oyster sauce, and sugar. Continue cooking for 5-7 minutes, stirring frequently.
7. Garnish with fresh cilantro and serve.

Iranian Tahchin

Ingredients:

- 2 cups basmati rice
- 1 lb chicken breasts, cooked and shredded
- 1 onion, finely chopped
- 1/2 cup plain yogurt
- 1/4 cup saffron water (soaked saffron in warm water)
- 1/4 cup vegetable oil
- 2 eggs, beaten
- 1/4 cup barberries (optional)
- 1 tsp turmeric
- Salt and pepper to taste

Instructions:

1. Cook the rice until tender, then drain and set aside.
2. Sauté the onions in oil until golden, then add the shredded chicken, turmeric, salt, and pepper.
3. In a separate bowl, combine the yogurt, saffron water, eggs, and salt.
4. Mix the cooked rice and yogurt mixture, then layer the bottom of a pot with the rice and top with the chicken mixture.
5. Cover and cook over low heat for 45 minutes to an hour, allowing the crust to form.
6. Optionally, top with sautéed barberries and serve.

Dominican Mangu with Rice

Ingredients:

- 2 green plantains, peeled and sliced
- 2 tbsp butter
- 1/4 cup olive oil
- 1 cup white rice, cooked
- 1 onion, thinly sliced
- 2 cloves garlic, minced
- 1/4 cup vinegar
- 1 tsp oregano
- Salt and pepper to taste

Instructions:

1. Boil the plantains in salted water until tender, about 15-20 minutes.
2. Mash the plantains with butter, olive oil, and a little water to achieve a smooth consistency.
3. In a separate skillet, sauté onions and garlic until soft, then stir in vinegar, oregano, salt, and pepper.
4. Serve the mangu with cooked rice and the sautéed onions on top.

Senegalese Thiéboudienne

Ingredients:

- 2 cups jasmine rice
- 1 lb fish (such as red snapper or tilapia), cleaned and cut into chunks
- 2 tomatoes, chopped
- 1 onion, chopped
- 1 bell pepper, chopped
- 2 garlic cloves, minced
- 2 tbsp tomato paste
- 1/2 cup vegetable oil
- 1 tsp cayenne pepper (optional for heat)
- 1/2 tsp thyme
- Salt to taste
- Fresh parsley for garnish

Instructions:

1. In a large pot, heat oil and sauté onions, bell pepper, and garlic until softened.
2. Add the tomatoes, tomato paste, cayenne pepper, and thyme. Stir and cook for 5-7 minutes.
3. Add the fish pieces, salt, and enough water to cover the fish. Simmer for 15-20 minutes.
4. Stir in the rice, cover with water, and cook for another 20-25 minutes until the rice is fully cooked and the flavors have melded.
5. Garnish with fresh parsley and serve.

Indian Lemon Rice

Ingredients:

- 2 cups basmati rice, cooked
- 1/2 cup peanuts, roasted
- 1/4 cup oil
- 1 tsp mustard seeds
- 1/2 tsp turmeric powder
- 1/2 tsp cumin seeds
- 1 green chili, chopped (optional)
- 1 tbsp fresh lemon juice
- Salt to taste
- Fresh cilantro for garnish

Instructions:

1. Heat oil in a pan and add mustard seeds, cumin seeds, and turmeric powder. Cook for 1 minute until fragrant.
2. Stir in the green chili and peanuts.
3. Add the cooked rice and toss to coat.
4. Stir in the lemon juice and salt, and cook for another 2 minutes.
5. Garnish with fresh cilantro and serve.

Guatemalan Arroz con Pollo

Ingredients:

- 2 cups long-grain rice
- 1 lb chicken (bone-in or boneless), cut into pieces
- 1 onion, chopped
- 1 bell pepper, chopped
- 2 garlic cloves, minced
- 1 cup tomatoes, chopped
- 1/4 cup tomato paste
- 1 cup chicken broth
- 1/2 cup peas and carrots (frozen or fresh)
- 1 tsp cumin
- 1 tsp paprika
- 1/2 tsp turmeric (for color)
- Salt and pepper to taste
- Fresh cilantro for garnish

Instructions:

1. In a large pot, brown the chicken pieces on all sides over medium heat. Remove and set aside.
2. In the same pot, sauté onions, bell peppers, and garlic until soft.
3. Stir in the tomatoes, tomato paste, cumin, paprika, turmeric, salt, and pepper.
4. Add the rice and chicken broth. Stir to combine, then add the browned chicken back into the pot.
5. Cover and cook on low heat for 25-30 minutes, or until the rice is cooked and the chicken is tender.
6. Stir in peas and carrots and cook for an additional 5 minutes.
7. Garnish with fresh cilantro and serve.

Turkish Rice with Spices

Ingredients:

- 2 cups basmati rice
- 1 onion, chopped
- 2 tbsp butter
- 1 tsp cinnamon
- 1/2 tsp cumin
- 1/2 tsp black pepper
- 1 1/2 cups chicken or vegetable broth
- Salt to taste
- Fresh parsley for garnish

Instructions:

1. Rinse the rice until the water runs clear, then soak it for about 15 minutes.
2. In a pan, melt butter over medium heat and sauté onions until golden.
3. Add cinnamon, cumin, and black pepper, stirring for 1 minute to release the aromas.
4. Add the soaked rice and sauté for 2-3 minutes to coat the grains with the spices.
5. Pour in the broth and bring to a simmer. Reduce the heat to low, cover, and cook for 15-18 minutes.
6. Let the rice sit covered for 5 minutes before fluffing with a fork.
7. Garnish with fresh parsley and serve.

Chinese Sticky Rice Dumplings (Zongzi)

Ingredients:

- 2 cups glutinous (sticky) rice
- 8-10 bamboo leaves, soaked in warm water for 30 minutes
- 1/2 lb pork belly or chicken, cut into chunks
- 2-3 dried mushrooms, soaked
- 2 tbsp soy sauce
- 1 tbsp sesame oil
- 1 tbsp oyster sauce
- 1 tsp five-spice powder
- 1/2 tsp white pepper
- Salt to taste

Instructions:

1. Soak the sticky rice for at least 2 hours or overnight.
2. In a pan, sauté pork or chicken chunks with soy sauce, sesame oil, oyster sauce, five-spice powder, white pepper, and salt for 5-7 minutes.
3. To assemble the dumplings, place a bamboo leaf flat, spoon a layer of rice onto it, then add a piece of pork or chicken and a mushroom. Top with more rice.
4. Fold the bamboo leaf into a triangle or rectangle shape to encase the rice and filling.
5. Tie each dumpling with string and steam for 1-2 hours until the rice is tender.
6. Serve warm.

Malaysian Sambal Rice

Ingredients:

- 2 cups jasmine rice, cooked
- 1 tbsp sambal oelek (chili paste)
- 1 tbsp soy sauce
- 1/2 tsp sugar
- 1/2 cup fried shallots
- 1/4 cup fresh cilantro, chopped
- 1 boiled egg, sliced (optional)

Instructions:

1. In a small bowl, mix the sambal oelek, soy sauce, and sugar until combined.
2. In a large pan, heat a little oil and sauté the cooked rice for 2-3 minutes.
3. Stir in the sambal sauce mixture and cook for another 3-4 minutes.
4. Garnish with fried shallots, fresh cilantro, and boiled egg slices (optional).
5. Serve hot.

Syrian Rice Pilaf

Ingredients:

- 2 cups basmati rice
- 1/4 cup butter or olive oil
- 1 onion, chopped
- 1 cinnamon stick
- 1/4 cup pine nuts, toasted
- 1/4 cup almonds, sliced
- 3 cups chicken broth
- Salt to taste
- Fresh parsley for garnish

Instructions:

1. Rinse the rice until the water runs clear, then soak it for 20 minutes.
2. In a large pot, heat butter or olive oil and sauté onions until golden.
3. Add the cinnamon stick and cook for 1-2 minutes.
4. Stir in the rice and cook for 2-3 minutes until lightly toasted.
5. Add the chicken broth and salt, then bring to a boil. Cover and simmer on low for 15-20 minutes until the rice is cooked.
6. Garnish with toasted pine nuts, sliced almonds, and fresh parsley.

Ukrainian Rice with Mushrooms

Ingredients:

- 2 cups long-grain rice
- 1/2 lb fresh mushrooms, sliced
- 1 onion, chopped
- 1 tbsp butter
- 1 1/2 cups vegetable broth
- 1 tsp thyme
- Salt and pepper to taste

Instructions:

1. Rinse the rice and cook according to package instructions.
2. In a skillet, melt butter and sauté the onions and mushrooms until soft and golden.
3. Add the thyme, salt, and pepper, and cook for another 5 minutes.
4. Stir the cooked rice into the mushroom mixture, adding vegetable broth if needed to keep it moist.
5. Cook for another 5 minutes, then serve.